As the reader of this book, I would like to thank you, with a pleasant and gracious gratitude, for purchasing my book!

"Thank You!"

You have helped me in ways that before just writing it's self could not. In a world built on economic status the hardest thing is attempting to be the "who am I" in the grand scheme of life factor. This catharsis poetry is how it all began for me. (Please note the simplicity in the presented writings that directly contributed to my self-development. Although there are a many creative writings in this small chapbook the bulk came from purging my soul; so to speak.

My name is Brandon J. Holland. I was born in MO, but raised in Muskegon, MI.

There is an interesting story behind that: My grand-mother died, she ejected through the center of a windshield into the grill of a semi-truck, when my mother was four years old and my mother was left with, well, I do not know, because I never really had a relationship with my mother. Seat belts were a great invention, but unfortunately not taken seriously in the sixties. Anyways, my mother crash landed in Muskegon, MI under the wing of my father. She was fifteen years old and my good o' father was thirty eight. He knocked her up, and she was a ward of the state of MI. She was left taking a bus back to MO, where she was born, to keep me from foster care. That is how I came about.

I do not think my mother ever knew what a good man was, because she never had a functional relationship. This includes with her children.

She says she always did the best she could, but I was raised as protector and man of the house until ten years of age when I was sent to live with my father; in which I had not known since three years old.

1

When I say protector I mean she always had abusive boyfriends and I would have to literally protect my family. You can take it from there.

I went to live with my father at ten, because my mother's newest boyfriend was the new dominant male in the house and was, very, threatened by the competition he felt from my presence. He was just another man to me, because loving her was a high turn-over job. There was none by the way I would just try to protect my mother, little sister, and little brother when adults were fighting around us. This fighting consisted of death threats, physical violence, and vile verbal abuse.

My father was the worst of the scenario and I unfortunately did not make it out of this relationship with any expectations at all. He taught his children (my older half-brother, older half-sister, and all of their friends) that it was a great thing to drink alcohol, smoke cigarettes, and use drugs.

I tried to go back to my mother's but she did not let me, because things had not cooled down. At least living with my mother I knew what to expect. She asked me what has happened to make me want to go back with her. Just before walking out the door my father said if I said anything about what goes on in the house that there would not be a home for me to come back to. I said nothing out of fear of what he would do to me, and the fear of abandonment and keeping my mother, little brother and sister safe.

Before this, there were no secrets in life. As my mother and I were sitting on the beach in her car, I asked her what she had in her cup and she told me seven and seven. I knew it was alcohol, because she always drank. I grabbed the cup and gulped it down and she took me back to my father's house. Before I got out I asked if it was going to make everything better for them that I stay with my dad and she said yes. The door shut on my life after that. I did not know which way was up or down. At the age of ten, I was using drugs such as; cocaine, weed, inhalants, alcohol, cigarettes, and exposed to sex by my father. He would bring women home from bars and have sex with them practically right in front of us. Some of his girlfriends would hit on my older brother and me, and show us their genitals. I knew in my heart it was all wrong, but the breaking point was when I found out about my older half-sister. She tried to kiss me and I freaked out. She said dad does it and we have sex, and I said this is wrong. She responded with sex is cool and it feels good too.

I was ten and there was no turning back.

To all of them associated with this house sex, drugs, and alcohol was a great thing. I stayed up that night with the crossbow in my hand, that my father bought me at the local flea market in Muskegon, MI, and lurked in the dark. I had him timed. Every night he would get out of bed to go pee at around midnight. Here he comes out of his slumber. I knew he was coming, because he always woke himself up with that wretched smokers cough. I held the cross bow up, but, just then my heart beating through my chest and breathing rapidly, as I was aiming it at his back I started to shake and I could not pull the trigger. Self-development was dead for the first time in my life, but later I found it would not be the last.

Life became a blur when I became helpless.

I did not wake up again until I had a son at the old street thug age of twenty. My life expectancy then was to die or be in prison by the time I hit twenty six. I am twenty nine now, thanks to my first born, learning from people's presentation of exterior selves, and what I call catharsis poetry.

Since 2001, three months after my son was born and eighteen days after 9/11 I was charged as a felon, because I felt there was immediate threat every-where. I was a drug dealer, and our nation was being attacked by terrorist, so I began carrying a weapon. I was caught by police with a forty four magnum and fleeing and eluding in my Chevy Monte Carlo. From this point on I began learning a new life style visually seen and felt through the empowered personification of the personnel in our judicial system. I watched people everywhere I was and pretended they were presidents, doctors, and rocket scientist even if they were crack addicts. I paved my own future through pretending and advice from professionals under the self-stricken pretense that anything is possible. Today I still play by the same rules, but I have evolved slightly into maturity and social clarity.

I have written several more additions to this book that I pray you will know as quality poetry, two adult drama theatrical performances, a children's theatrical performance, a children's book series, numerous invention blueprints, and I am working on several fantasy/fiction novels. But, this book was the foundation of my new life and I hope that you see this as you read. Good luck and God speed lovely patrons and pray for my success in the entertainment industry as another positive entity.

With Love,

Forgotten Me Ink Co.

Emotional Primal Evolution

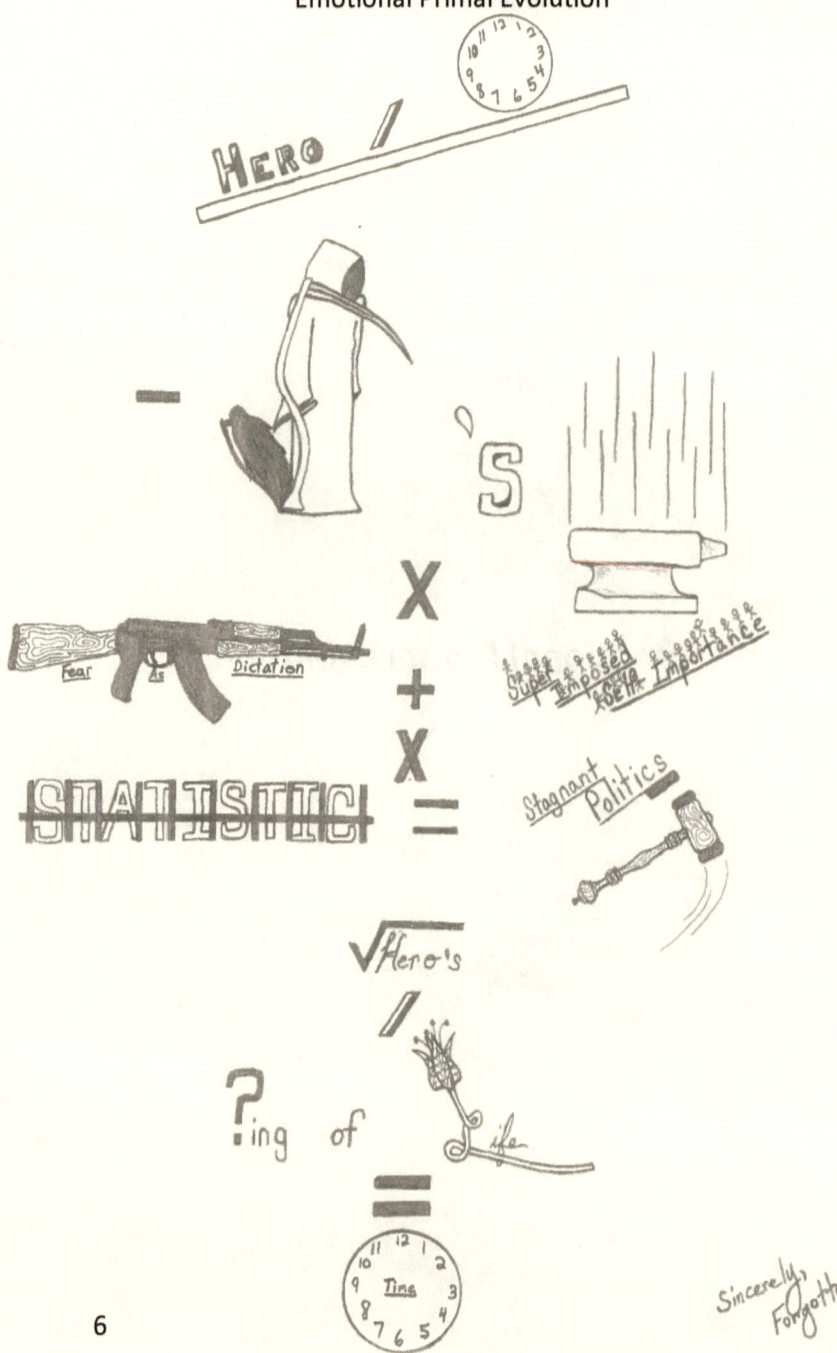

Just Wondering

So, I was thinking about the origin of epiphanies,
revolutionaries, diseases bodies carry, and a single
man having 100 concubines to carry his ego lavishly.

My ideal, perceptions on reality, is that it can never
be reckoned leaving it to me a twist fetish.

All the while, maybe life is not a question.

Maybe it is a thing that neither you nor I can
understand.

This is where and when man's poetry began.

As the heart of man/woman felt their first hurt and
words started to listen with a subtle collision; it
brought forth intellectual competition.

The beckon call brings to life many plans.

"To live and be life" is our most prized forgotten
innovation; evolution of euphoric apprehension.

Excluding indicted domination in suspended
sensational surrealism, legal legislation, or target
marketing in corporate segregation.

Emotional Primal Evolution

We out smart ourselves, with ignorance as smarts opposed to brain meets the heart.

When as, everything that is ripe and pure, begins with strength and endurance maturing through life ending in quenching revelation while decaying in decollation.

What was once young an innocent is now, modernisms plaque, misguided ill visions.

Sincerely,

Forgotten Me (An Isolated Condemnation)

Stabilities Rocker

I shout rage to the world from the highest points.

Only breathing air that thins the blood to faintness and doubling in pints.

To cities and wilderness, I give the indigenous seed conceiving ears, striking blows through heart and

mind with epiphanies preserved there in nothingness,
but nothingness there in exuding every-thing.

I am exerting these, vulgar and vile, inflamed feelings
of restlessness from people's anti-humane attitudes of
plenty.

In it all, I know there is more, but the world has only
shown me to be less.

Fear is what collapses the mind at an early age.

Panic filled me with aimless rage hazed in the
burning sage.

Taking the right of childhood away and placed in an
abusive indictive cage.

Statistical education is only to be me lost in a page of
a docile play never staged.

These are the words from a victim of tragedy fed
into the chaos to be another number lived without a
name.

The years have been far too long, ravaging horror to
all physical, but my mind is still so strong.

Emotional Primal Evolution

Now I see clear, my time is growing near, so I will stand my ground when tyranny sounds.

I am the means of means.

Cessation of a life that should never be given as a blessing, for this I am firmly here.

When my knees try to buckle, I will not coward with fear.

Now the tress I see, I can't recognize even with my blind eye.

This is a bold new world, and a bold new climb.

The confusion sets all at the same space in time on the eroding realities eluding my minds cry.

I feel only the dying core.

Every moment is transitional, but my utterances of incompetence are surged words when I implore.

All around me the trees, I've seen, the vibrant forest once cherished in my adolescent memories are crushed to the floor.

When I try to blend I can chameleon no more.

Emotional Primal Evolution

The rose petals once silky to my touch are now flaky from decay and the betrayal of trust.

My self-preservation has become the ill dedication of this repetitious daily lives, lazy nation.

Liberation of one's self requires application.

If I do not imply to apply I'll be lost in the devastation.

Can I cage my ambition?

I am here, yet, my non-existence sputters then re-ignites my ignition.

This parallel intuition is burning lighting my path poised and reluctant.

In the same instant, I'm a ghost writer or soul quenching, barely breaking sound, musical note telling the heart peace is a grasp from being existent.

Can I cage my ambitions?

Lock my mind in a box to dismay, discontinuing my mission.

Is it even my decision to cage these ambitions?

Emotional Primal Evolution

Sincerely,

Forgotten Me

Putting Me On Hold

There is confusion on the receiving end and this cord
will not extend in the way I need it to bend.

Causing these mixed emotions from the love, tones,
and tension with this conversation failing to blend.

You're part of me and your essence more than a
friend.

You are sweet rolling lush green pastures I bloom inn.

This particular situation within conversation
prosperity has yet fallen.

When there the golden rays of sun that once brightly
gleamed, providing life through the U.V. beams are,
now, interrupting harmonic balance, and in an
instantaneous second, turned these pastures burnt

brown instead of vibrant green and white lily of the valley.

The cord is not long enough the way I need it to bend.

It's hot then cold, as the wind hits with battling quarrels.

Mixed emotions cause my shoreline to dispute and tsunamis crash in an unknown world.

Your mentality has put me on hold, like a rubber band wrapped tightly around my frontal lobe.

I feel stuttered, stumbled, choked up, and as a sealed glass bottle aching to explode from being rapidly transferred from hot to cold.

Your lack of compassionate expression in this conversation has kinked my hose.

Then you abruptly put me hold.

I am left battling self-control looking out a bullet proof glass window.

Sincerely,

Forgotten Me

Healing Consuming Her Time

Born in hell is what the papers will say.

I was raised in hell; hell bound but not by choice.

For this I will fight the coy and posture my poise;
simple words lead only to more noise.

My own thoughts are my muse, because the forefront
of reality is as, plainly seen, the ingesting of gasoline.

Another world and time, because this life I do not
belong; by a fast many I will stifle with the sounding
gong.

Three to every one year passes when my birthday
comes and slips, again, to the lonely gallows.

Emotional Primal Evolution

The hell hounds disrupt my information interpreting process, in light of Maslow, making my days hot to the touch living chaotic and short.

There are no walls big enough to kill necessities social inertia, me to you; vice versa.

The hour hand moves faster than minutes.

My pathway is set in stone geared toward harm with no escort.

It's dark and lonely here where these sunglasses are televisions and I am watching black hail and gloom.

God's scent sent me to you, of another world, to become the only rose that blooms in this room.

Self-centered and misconstrewed, I became the rain cloud fierce, relentless, and showing no remorse.

Even God's hand cannot help men when man is a free moral decisions tomb.

Her bloom is hung half dead from struggling to stay through seeds of faith and knowledge that all friction will take its course.

Emotional Primal Evolution

Her beauty hangs in the balance while I push her out with the tremor force of a sonic boom.

Yet, I claim I love her.

Conceived in hell is what the papers will say.

A man's sanity is the questioning of an insane world, because I was raised in hell, but not by choice.

My own thoughts are the muse in which my reality is placed on the forefront of a plainly seen in-gestation of gasoline.

The light to my darkness, and I was pushing her away.

The day to my night, but my cloud would not give way.

There was never enough rain for her to regain the tears she gave.

No words can express the gratitude and my feelings for you.

The years of your sacrifice, was Christly to me, and I now see more than my own battles.

Emotional Primal Evolution

Our days grow longer, holding tight to you, with joys contentment, dark into light, and love into bloom.

She is the only rose in my room.

Overwhelmed by corruption, love has acquainted me to another way of life.

The rehabilitation of ill-mannered dedication consumed me in connection to my vile past being disregarded dragged so far out of life living context.

On the heels of God's scent, she was quickly found and made my new vest of, beyond my heavenly cling, inner peace, shelter, and confidence.

I can now smile, here and there, although haunted forever by a lethally hindering hex.

In-which, the only justification has the requisite, co-figuratively perplex, to live so insanely complex.

There is new wind in my hair, giving me a new chair, carried by the rose begat from strife.

She is the tingle to my stoned heart, now one day to be my wife.

She will always and forever be, be a God's scent, the only rose in my life.

Sincerely,

Forgotten Me

<u>*Loving Tender Breeze*</u>

I am the eagle wings, my legs stout as trees.

The wind in my hair, sun to my back, and sand on my feet render me free.

Yet, all this beauty cannot pull me from the conflict in peace.

Day inn and night out, continuously, I wish to anything, animal or human being, listening with feeling.

I wish that I could wisp away as sleek as the breeze to kiss the day.

It would not be a job; just a happening.

Then I am off at any given second and in any different direction.

Like a breeze freely flowing relentlessly through fields and forest.

Whistling and howling weaving in and out of endless trees.

Gathering the vapors, I would caress waves across huge bodies of lakes, oceans, and seas.

Helping dolphins fly those extra freestyle feet.

Helping birds on their travels for that extra speed.

If I were the wind every day would have a breath taking end, and a glorious new dawn beginning.

Every living species legged, finned or winged would with every view of their lives remember it to be refreshing.

Every crack and clevis, crick and creek, every nation ruled by the people, king, and queen, and through the mountainous ranges to the highest peaks would always have a fitting breeze blowing.

Emotional Primal Evolution

If I were the wind I would flourish all that is good,
every day, more and more, I would.

Thrusting and piercing away, like a soldier's bayonet,
all that bothers us within.

Therein, harm and bad things would matter to us the
least.

One short somber sweet whisper and corruption,
money, and thinking I can change the world would
cease, and no longer give us grief.

Moreover, if I were given the chance, well, I know I
could fill the shoes of the breeze.

Given the chance I wonder what others wish they
could be.

Sincerely,

Forgotten Me

Hate In Love-Love In Hate

Desperately sewn unto you; it seems.

I am thunderously fierce with inevitable truth.

I have taken the sun and the moon, bringing this body to ashes and dust, for the wind to perfume and mysteriously, but true, you have become the only light in my room.

I do not know if I deserve this blessing, because I am nothing more than a self-guided, self-consumption timed to end in a huge plume.

Rather I should say, a kamikaze dying off mistakes in a plummet of self-center, so called, good deeds.

Which is, as seen in my eyes, is deflowering my rose turning her into a weed.

This sand storm of couth is turning my heart cold excepting less in life, losing confidence, and turning my head from the oversight of devilish deeds instead of debating and recreating these ill rooted trees.

Vigilante of a new bread doomed from the conception of the seed.

Emotional Primal Evolution

My mind is collapsed by hearts necessity; the light of my life and the smile to my strife.

The deception and confusion of lust mixed in the dedication of love has brought me to the sharp side of a knife.

I have lost everything that matters soully to my maintain.

Did I lose it to illusions frame, or good deeds without a name?

Or did I lose it to this poetry written with pure passion, but continues to be self-portrayed in vain of sadness glissading on falling rain.

My confidence is hung shame.

Confusion attempts to make me feel as if I am at blame.

Chaos into idle, idle into chaos, chaos into enlightenment, enlightenment into good, good into introspection, and introspection into this; why will there never be bliss?

Leaving on a smooth ride, but led straight through rough terrain.

Emotional Primal Evolution

Whether up or down this life has become distant and hard to claim.

I am now paused in a place.

Where is it?

It seems to be more of what cannot be seen by the face.

Sincerely,

Forgotten Me

Prey And Predator

If I am a wolf of a rare majestic silhouette I would be deep in wood lands of raw nature.

I could never be fully understood by humanity.

I would always to be known as a carnivorous crusader; a nomad flesh feeding flock raider.

Emotional Primal Evolution

My only biography at the thick of an old oak would be a worn told tail for the finding.

Under the tree a home in a hole was dug.

The ceiling is made up of a two century old tree.

Blanketed on the floor of the den would be soften remains of rotting roots, there for bedding, insolating the mud.

Matts of fur found clasped to wood spurs.

Pools of water gather in divots with lining of past seasons left debris.

If I am labeled a modern wolf; the mysterious, vicious, carnivorous crusader that seeks blood, than inner me, I would be an instinctual, swarming, sea.

Given the decisions of today, given to me in accordance by the laws of up-holding societal dignity, I would be inoperable; mentally incompetent to be.

In this canine scenario, if I am a wolf on the unjustifiable judging spot held by your selection of faces would be torn flesh and your lungs, still trying desperately to breath from the ongoing feeding frenzy, would slowly flood with blood.

Emotional Primal Evolution

My principle would be to eat the likes of you, because the sickly (ill-guided warranting) lean to the herd or group for strength.

Struggling at this game in survival of the fittest, you try to catch up to everyone, but stray.

Because your weak being secluded into selfish self-loathing and greed.

Sacrifice for the better is an acceptance and state of mind; instead you plead.

The humble are the strong for, as a whole, they stick together.

The wolf, in all its glorious grandeur, has no conscience.

Then, rightfully, through existence I become the hunter.

To kill for the wolf in the wilderness means he or the bitch will not have to do it again until the next cycle passes.

But for me to do as the label proceeds me to be, my job would be continuous with no remorse and having no conscience.

Therein, this would not be nothing spectacular or genius.

Justifiable for I am the product of humanity with the premises; therein, being raised in and by said society.

This gives me the ability to decide when wrong from right clashes.

There lay justification of wrong action leading to just provocation.

The wolf I am proclaimed to be will give equal in pain to the oppressors.

This is for what you willingly bestowed on another living being for self-amusement at your convenience.

Thus, on that grey and gloomy, pulse booming night a horse will ride in, fit for battle, but the wolf, of inner me, will rightfully collect the dues and tithe of unjust deceivers and deliver the bite.

Then, flash backs will be given to you where you lie.

This is an inheritance from the earth's recollect conscience.

She will bring forth the equal vision and pain that you changed innocence into suffering vain, and played god for one or more instances to deny lives sublime existence.

Sincerely,

Forgotten Me

How Many Tears Can a Doll Cry?

The eternal beckoned call has rang, and what was perfect together is expressed in one's displace in loss.

Where-as, life to another, but fates thumb enchanted thirty six years to live forever.

His clean shaven touch and spice in numerous plies would smother miraculously lift her clutter.

On the day of reckoning an ear grabs a distant whisper, "ca cah", as the gentle brush of together, filled the touch to her face by a communing feather flights flutter, watching the last moments lowering her lost.

Still present in touch, essence, and sight to hearts love there was no true dispatcher, but tonight she lay in restless slumber, throwing her arm over the empty shell of the cover.

Tears on Jazmyn's cheek fall every night on all lovers.

A journey in melancholy to know tomorrow will bring more.

Alone, living captured memories by day and setting the table for two by moonlight.

Friends and family can only watch saying she does it to herself, to move on, that she's youthful and of a precious commodity, rare, only to adore.

Then, one days end, with a black to gold, glissading, to an arraying pearl rainbow purple pelt, a crow's "ca cahs" on the left perch of her front door.

This bird behaves peculiar, she thought, as it cahed in a low voice and nodded its head up and down as she entered her home.

Emotional Primal Evolution

She checked to see if it was still there and as it spoke in a low roar she laid some sunflower seeds on the floor and said: well, I think you will make a nice décor.

She chuckled and walked in to bed.

What was an immortal day and endless night now absorbs her life.

A women somber and sweet, tasteful with grace and allure, became determined to not let forever drift to sea from shore.

Her heart was given as though tithe, and produced isolation, a loathly floating letter in the bottle, not letting go of her untouchable dream weighted by delusional strife.

Working until her bones hurt to the core, she arrives home to the friendly "ca cahs" of the crow roosting at her front door.

I just fed you just yesterday; you must like the seeds and my you are becoming a handsome bird.

She would say to the bird, and the bird would stay.

Jazmyn has a new friend in play.

Silent prayers holding her love as she lay her head to regenerate for another day in the same.

She wakes every day with the lamed claim, to complete another day in her perception of her loss's ideal respective.

She would work in the garden and the lovely, glissading, and sound full bird would hop on her back and nibble at her hair hopping down and steeling more, purposely placed, sunflower seeds from her gardening apron.

Day to day she has become connected to the crow's loyal "ca cahs".

She began to believe the bird a medium with intention to communicate.

She would always listen intently.

Filling her void like it's there on behalf of the only one to open her gate.

He did have such a beautiful song.

She lay comforted hidden in her cove sheltered from another's affection or illusions from the beauty when two fuse, and at the door her reality guarding protector for recollect Jazmyn's former, present, and periodic hope of him returning completing their promise of forever is her only incentive.

Five years slipped lucidly where five left off of two companion's singer through a messenger in distant song.

Then one day the crow's time had come and gone, because it was never truly there all along.

As her day came to an end now feeling disconnected from everything, her mind stilled to the portrait of her heart, time turned existence divine as Jazmyn floated away with just breaking dawn.

Sincerely,

Forgotten Me

Question

If I have one question that cannot be answered, am I wronged?

Did I not ask the question loud enough?

Was the clarity not met with measure?

Maybe it was not meant to be answered.

To right to know; like the words have not yet matured.

Yet, maturity is questionable enough, as all acts are dissected for debate, and it having any pretense to this question has made it wrong, already.

O' question, o' question in my heart, please answer me when the wind blows.

Why have you weighed on me so?

My mind is under lock and key.

Only your answer can set me free.

Reveal some hint or clue that I should know.

I feel wronged from this unanswered question indeed.

Emotional Primal Evolution

Did I not answer the question loud enough?

Was the clarity not met with measure?

Maybe it was not meant to be answered.

To right to know; like the words have not yet matured.

Yet, maturity is questionable enough, as all acts are dissected for debate, and it having any pretense to this question has made it wrong, already.

O' question, o' question, o' question in my mind; please answer me from the blue water timed wave chimes.

Why do you render me emotionally, mentally, and physically blind?

Your importance has compelled me, like it is only and always been you, and I have been placing I in team.

My persona hangs in the balance of a finger-tip over delete to the cost of your tentative fee.

Your o' suddenly I am here introductory I wish there were a more formal blood spilling.

Emotional Primal Evolution

To answer you has become my daily grind.

Another year has come under your cloak and sheen.

I swear it is dictation over poetic me, but all outside
sees is physical beauty.

O' please someone break this tyranny; I breathe in
quiet chi.

Inside I am bubbling over, unfastened, lightly at loft
as a pheasant falling.

O' am I not asking the question loud enough?

Maybe it was not meant to be answered.

To right to know; like the words have not yet
matured.

Yet, maturity is questionable enough, as all acts are
dissected for debate, and it having any pretense to
this question has made it wrong, already.

O' question, o' questioning seeming just out of my
reach, at times I am lost trying to learn from the
ways you teach.

Emotional Primal Evolution

You claim blood and I bleed attempting to live you as though you are me.

You are not physically true.

Yet, my mind makes you powerful and therein you reign.

I am the vessel through which you come unglued.

In the brood of my mind you boil stagnantly crude.

I now understand our correlation, that with-out you, my conscience of lives pursuits, my world would be chaos and under siege.

You answered is me.

Sincerely,

Forgotten Me

Space In Time As A Minute Of Mine

I have this minute; this minute in time.

To slow this minute down, in spatial rhyme, would truly make this a minute of mine.

I see the horizon, an infinite line, and I am trying to capture this moment before daylight is consumed by night.

The sun kissed sky, from my Muskegon sight, is fading dark blue to pink.

It is still cold being late February, and I remain here, frigid and a devilishly handsome daring man.

Then it is cut with clouds darkly shadowed forming a mountainous picket line dropping into Lake Michigan.

Mini ice bergs bobbing like little seals appear ready to dine.

This is my minute, and I am soaking the last rays of sunshine.

Satisfying, yet a little disappointing, this in particular as the sun makes it is daily plummet.

Emotional Primal Evolution

If there were someone on the Wisconsin side he or she could throw a stone to cause a big enough hole in the clouds so I can see the last of it.

Then I could quench the deepest thirst in this minute.

The colors are slowly diminishing and my minute you are ticking away.

But, oh yes, indulging in you has, o' suddenly, very pleasantly made the stars come flaming out winking bright on your midnight suit.

Yes, ah yes, I see you.

Every-one is brighter than the next.

Deep in me there is a part wishing that deep in space a super nova explodes showing its chest.

The time passes and one by one you are burning stout in your permanent crest.

A new minute has achieved; indeed.

So deep into a sensual moment it is hard to remember, but memory is forced having the force of a minute as equal to the sun giving my very existence.

Emotional Primal Evolution

It is time to kiss the sky goodbye a kiss this beautiful minute of mine until we fly.

Sincerely,

Forgotten Me

Blinded

Destruction has come, and its orientation is known verses unknown to recollect or seeing eyes perception.

The rebuilding is now taking place, but yesterday was too short for memories collection.

Why this pain that hurts both pleasantly and petulantly from the buildings resurrection.

Yesterday's havoc was confusions hurtful guild prodding my mind with no absolution or even clarity from and in conception.

Relentless chaos so tomorrow there is something to work for?

Emotional Primal Evolution

Dedication in a sense is destruction.

Destruction is only no self-control self-combustion.

Stuck in contemplation of Forgotten Me verses
exterior self is now added by in the midst of
confusions ennoble cause, a third party.

I let you co-exist with my genetics synaptics.

In-turn, I am halted in hypothesis of, seemingly my
own, exclusive situations.

My most important thought is how I am going to
reach the mentally tiresome destination.

I let you cloud my whole, individual personality, lives
visualization.

I am troubled now by blind hate and induced ill-wit
as the way I am shown to disperse my sweaty
consummation.

Work for you, work for him, or work for them
dropping me into a boiling pot of irrational
processing.

Emotional Primal Evolution

Another day is lost due to my humility being of a
higher cause, than objective living, self-subjection to
erratic distracting compilations.

Or is it self-conceded greed I am exploiting.

The stress of these impulsive selfish self-contradictions
of expectations and interactions has left me of
valence unbalanced chemical reactions.

No longer am I able to find myself in myself.

I have lost my own voice and course of action.

Aimless rage fills me and chills my heart consuming
every interaction in a furious fashion.

Sharp and short vocal vibes dictates the composition
few, far, and in-between the lines in conversation.

These little moments are the illusive pest that
burrows under my skin to nest is milliseconds not yet
mastered in literal depiction by my poetic millisecond
spy's illustration.

Another's words are my only natural enemy until I
decode the real messages.

Now I am left in a non-improvable situation with no way out, but one syllable meditations.

What have I become?

Sincerely,

Forgotten Me

Interrogation Of Myself

Insomnia is the ory introspection to all between me and me in the mirror.

Everything I understand myself to be is the reflection of my daily life in the mirror.

There is a spatial barrier of energy that separates me between the projections of myself in the mirror.

So, me in the mirror is who I am, standing in front of the mirror is my physical presence, and between me and the mirror is the physical presence and psyche projection of all others in the world.

Emotional Primal Evolution

Therefore, there are three dimensions of reality.

My interpretation of the third dimension is the verbalization; I call poetry, of human energy.

Poetry is an obligation, forms of written, expressions from living relations, to our most individual feelings.

It is the story of successes contrasted by failures and once upon a time, the sacrifice of true lives, life completing.

It is the space in time, without time, and portrait of the motions in seamless rhyme.

Poetry is a blind man explaining, in pictorial words as hand gestures almost quicken to a blur, what he was once given through the perception of visual conception.

Poetry is instantaneous, strategic, and erratically captured by my millisecond spy.

It is a smile from a total stranger, for the first time, since his mother found what it was to die; as he walks bye.

Poetry is the obvious influence of mothers eye shot look through child's conduit.

Emotional Primal Evolution

It is a psychological mathematical feud of unexpressed interpersonal entangled changes, chances, choices, and personal differences.

Poetry is opening a caged door interrupting ignorance being bliss; moreover, being freed from single-mindedness.

It is the liberation by revelation from a subliminal self-imprisonment to an imposed unwanted indictment; without joining a revolution.

Poetry is the culmination of a whole life in a few seconds just before a head on collision.

Poetry is the final decision of a life under the knife; totally leaping by faith in a prayer to the dependency of another person's precision.

It is the passionate heat love and hate brings cheap.

A confusion chain affecting a person's reality with vivid life front illusions, causing the mental evaluation to be incomprehensive colas' of thoughts twisted into a web of miss-illusion.

Poetry is every happening and wishes of what could have from origination to main point destination.

Emotional Primal Evolution

It is the air between you and me, and the simplicity in recreation.

Poetry is sporadic, signed with an easement to debate, and the purity is hard to dictate.

Poetry is being exceptive, receptive, and not selective intertwining with collective.

It is letting personal individuality and the divinity of creativity to joint.

Poetry is my mind in a spacious divide of a tumbling free axis triangle with no points.

Sincerely,

Forgotten Me

Binge

Most all can be noted incidental.

Emotional Primal Evolution

It will either be an abrupt change or slow developing systematic happening.

With every happening builds behavior and through the repetition behavior imprints and is addicting; continuously recreating its own reason for existing.

Incidentally noted everything can be corrected, relearned, or beaten, changed, and freed.

From the time I leave, disappear into my desolate retreat, I unconsciously recon sum you in the air I breathe.

You present yourself to be plankton in the sea; without you there could be no me.

My fill is never full for the day, I eat again, again, and again numbing my heart with self-defeat.

It seems to belong, like my fare ladies sweet somber song.

My heart palpitates, thumping through my chest, as though someone is massaging it with steel spiked prongs.

Everything is addicting, accordingly to severity, to the way I speak.

Emotional Primal Evolution

Here are some noted sporadically: the drugs I consume, the food I eat, spirits sweating through my pours, behaviors I repeat, and everything against the one I swear deity.

I am the friction of the hammer to the nail.

I am the wind in the sinking ships sail.

Every minute is transitional past, and I have many minutes.

What does it mean to lose one or two?

My minutes tick by every time I fail.

Now I know my indulging addicts call is my own tainted sweet betrayal.

It barks and I bite; as the wolf protecting its trail.

Every minute is transitional and therein I fail.

Sincerely,

Forgotten Me

Emotional Primal Evolution

To Live

A life inhabiting vessel not dying before it has fought
to live to let love live even be-latently loved lavishly.

Loosing You

What a gentle breeze that blows embracing
mysterious love.

The love gentle as I see, I know all too well, it can be
vicious seeking wrath through blood in the veins of
compatibility.

Like I have known it has stolen the flow.

My gentle breeze caressing gentle breeze you are;
where did you go?

There is no comfort in a world without the intangible.

Now, it is nature's pelting wind blow.

You left and it is cold, but not snow.

Emotional Primal Evolution

I catch, now, a still falling ash without a glow.

There is no swirly whirl and no side winding, loopy loop spiraling swirl.

You're gone and with your departure you have taken my whole world.

There is no wind to push the ash or this dreary.

I am now alone feeling I cannot be heard no matter the decibel query.

My dependency to you, breeze, kept me free.

Now, in a state of confusion, in my mind eyes vision I am blinded and yet, I can still see.

However, where there was a burst of wind, inevitability will bring a gust or two more for my quenching.

I will try to fret not.

So, I still love you breeze wherever you may be, but for this time, left in computations of past moral decisions, I must bare this ashy fate.

I will rise once more off these scarred knees.

Emotional Primal Evolution

This is a place where neither man nor woman should please.

A place caused by loves conquest combined with natures laws that nothing will be embraced in the arms of eternity.

I am left in a self-exploration masked by a bitter dependency that one day life will have me as its fee.

I forget about you and remember Forgotten Me, my inner dwelling individual, and begin to broaden my street mentality.

Again I am left with my optimistic chi to rebuild with a tangible nothing.

Nevertheless, these thoughts themselves must be blessings, because if not I would be enduring menacing eternal havoc with no smile to humility.

In this scenario there would never be another loving tender breeze blowing.

I am a soldier, but even the hardest crumble when attempting to bend at this degree.

This stretch of struggling trials and tribulations must mean something.

Emotional Primal Evolution

Why would I be living and enduring.

So, in and out of my purist purges of faith I shall keep my creed and keep thrusting.

I love you my breeze; you are everything.

Sincerely,

Forgotten Me

<u>Occupation Of The Mind</u>

When I think about the mind, there is not real sense of time.

There is only one thought and one action.

Multitasking is more of the same in a repetitious grind fashionably inclined.

There are no boundaries and boarders guarded by a line.

50

Emotional Primal Evolution

The thought to mind is mine guarded by frail flesh
and bridle bone engineered tragically fine.

Like a key to a lock this is only held true if they are
to combine.

But why the mind to human's ply?

Is the purpose to puzzle or to elude the chase?

Or is it to conclude all laying claims philosophical
clause of it and only iff fortifiable cased?

Is the design to reign over darkness to receive lime or
dreamless shine?

Therein, the mind that is not mine, and the mind I
am not to find am I to sights only taste.

There is no connection, but are connected very fine.

It is encrypted to our DNA's design.

In respects thereof, why does the mind that is not
mine directly paralyze my prime?

Maybe it is for power and greed, or iniquities blur
and parallel need.

It is entertaining to think that the mind can come to absolute answers when the only true answers are fingered delusional, because they are divine.

Sincerely,

Forgotten Me

My Shadow

It would seem time has run out for me, but for you it has just began to sing.

In my mind I see roads end veiled shimmer less, dark sheen as a dense consuming blanket of nothingness, loneliness, bitterness, and tensely condemning consumes.

What am I to do, because I have no brakes to halt me living for you?

Catharsis, I am the heir of nothingness, and it's shadow un-groomed.

Emotional Primal Evolution

Once branded golden child, but now my being is battered as Forgotten Me.

How awful the spin.

Freedom's past has grown putrid passing in to what was thought reconciliation, but now dimmed by aimless outrages of retaliation.

It seems the strength of heart can vanish as smoke to the wind.

This mind is, now, left in a dungeon, so to speak, alone only to imagine truth that has come unsown.

I can no longer see, not teachable in the respects of what I speak, because from birth all bad has been dealt and only glimpses of good have been seen.

I have been left in intrinsic thought to judge books by cover to what they seem.

My eyes are now shut and self-development is dead.

There is no reason for me to feel anything anymore or when nothing anymore is willing to feel for me in this state of unborn ultimatum casting dread.

Emotional Primal Evolution

I am a bird encaged feeling freedom, but only seeing it through tempered window.

Twenty six years old and life has already taken its toll.

I can only pray my story be told, but first I need you to understand something.

If you never take the time to know that enough is enough, then enough will never be enough.

You will never be satisfied knowing that enough will never be enough and you will never be kept full.

Sincerely,

Forgotten Me

My Family

In this decree all the salt has bled from this sea.

There are no more waves or current to ruffle debris.

Emotional Primal Evolution

With every thrust in the row lives determination leaves my stroke.

There is no more life to these providing waters, fresh and blue, in lay the mystery in me.

My olfactory once a gaped for the sweet fragrant crushes in the gentle breeze.

My tongued lips tease past pleasures of sun dried treats.

Now, there is no reality but the battle of inner me out bidding all other fallacies.

Therein, there is no extent and no extreme I would not go assuring your happiness.

Before you my days run their heat swallowed by the cold of the night.

Through the canvas you're sheen stole my sight as lightning struck witness.

Your arrival gave me reason for second life.

I love you, and I will never put anything above you; my nest.

Emotional Primal Evolution

No four walled shelter or haven, riches or stitches, could provide as much truth as to price.

This shackling of time where the old is always new spent in rhyme hand in hand, eye to eye, and chest to chest sang to a song of poetic invest.

Life has become my ultimate test.

Blind steps kept their distance when you opened your eyes.

Preserving your cries, laughs, freedom, and simple resilience proves my breath and makes it the best.

I am the ferry in this beckoning on looking my precious cargo manifest.

Therein, no longer am I void, a shelled crest, or hollowed chest.

My heart beats wildly like the rufous.

I am debited as my life next to yours is nothingness.

Moreover, in this decree new salt has bled into this sea.

There are more waves and current to ruffle debris.

Emotional Primal Evolution

With every thrust in the row lives determination replenishes new strokes.

There is now more life to these providing waters, fresh and blue, in lay the mystery in you.

My olfactory a gaped for the sweet fragrant crushes in the gentle breeze.

My tongued lips taste pleasures of sun dried treats.

Now, there is no reality but the battle of inner me out bidding all other fallacies.

When I fail you at times, blatant or hidden between the lines, to you it is not a sour deal.

My heart peels every mistake in apprehensions zeal, oh it feels, of the feel to a pain so forefront and real.

Even when everything has been said there are no words to describe the emotions left from each omission; like taking the hair from Salomon.

Each time it happens you lose a meal.

You are my devotional clarity and purity when all else is lost or I am trapped in time as Forgotten Me.

Emotional Primal Evolution

My existence is the preservation of your self-definition.

My life next to yours is nothing if you are firm standing, and only then do I live again in heaven.

I do not question that somehow I have been found in this incomparable bond of human to human.

The cause gives me self-greatness; your life for my death is contentment.

Resurrected from your love, any mental sway vestige makes my stomach twinge wishing for impalement.

I gladly give it for your lively existence.

Therein, if I am to fight, God is the light I will leap with faith into flight.

When my heart stops it will only start again a fire a million degrees hotter than the last.

You next to me cannot be whereas I have expired, and am left me next to you.

My seasons have already exuding pretentious presence.

Emotional Primal Evolution

I work hard nine to five in relentless persistence to sustain this warrant, and I give no resistance.

The flowing form of dedication illustrated from me to you is love being highest law.

This decree is made by the blood into the salt of this sea.

That there will, forevermore, be waves and current ruffling the debris.

With every thrust in the rows let life bring determination to the strokes.

In these providing waters, fresh and blue, lay the mystery for you to be tried and rang true.

Let your olfactory agape for the sweet fragrant crushes in the gentle breeze.

Tongue your lips tasting teasing pleasures of sun dried treats.

Let there be no reality but the battle of inner peace out bidding all other fallacies.

Therein, have no extent and no extreme you will not go assuring your families happiness.

Sincerely,

Forgotten Me

Cut The Chat

A prophet or philosopher I am not, but sure shot on the bull's eye dot you can bet the lot.

But, I can speak of your dreams as I can say they should be as mine; hot like boiling water in a small pot.

She is in it like me; dreams keep me going.

I was blessed only by the hand of God's doing.

I am from the gutter with a million to one odds showing.

A thorough bred from the ash and dust living barred statistics, but the wind keeps blowing.

Emotional Primal Evolution

I am buried under the drift, but my hands keep rowing.

I left planet earth to go ballistic, and severed myself from the streets and misfits.

Survival of the fit in which I have nothing except my courage, heart, and everything, but simplistic.

The system, sickly judicial moral value, left my back to the wall learning from the havoc.

Transparent to your show, I have nothing to mull.

All I had has been stripped and now I am willing to grab this paper to let it show.

I have an inexplicable talent to control time, in words, with mathematical parables.

Deeply divulge into what I am saying to you and you will to; start with positive ink, forget at first but finish knowing money is honey, and until then copyright dictation.

My mind is strong, and I will continue to shovel.

Emotional Primal Evolution

When times get tough I will rumble, and though I may stumble, crack, crumble the words fumble as I rise in good form the from ruble.

Above all, I will still comprehend the struggle.

I will live another day to join the cause of freedom.

This is a, carefully, conducted fight for liberties prism.

98.6 is just a statement, because the human heart burns a million degrees hotter.

Trust in your heart and you will find another way to school.

Sincerely,

Forgotten Me

Attributable Success

As I welcome myself back from insanities ledge, returning seems so soon.

Emotional Primal Evolution

The room still dims to black hail and gloom; my mind cannot disguise the truth.

The reality of the situation is that I cannot save societal couth, and for sanities sake I recant my eyes to recess.

Where the sun hit the sand dunes, and did so beautifully set just to the right where the cargo ships ported their manifest, coming through the channel at Pere Market.

The life here has given many lessons to which I have no regret.

Where the coal barges drag, the Lake Express glides, the Port City Princess slips, and the Highway 16 rest; I still myself in Ludington watching the Badger car-ferry press.

Just another proud town in Michigan and for these years I will now regress to the lite waves washing the shore, and the ten o'clock curfew horn sounding a lovely lullabies sweet caress.

These are the days my heart is at rest.

Emotional Primal Evolution

The next day opens and as I welcome myself back from the romp in my dreams, returning seems so soon.

Every day here seems to brighten my beckon calls of black hail and gloom.

I know I will forever see hell's flames on the roof in realities truth, but Ludington will always be my never ending moon.

Sincerely,

Forgotten Me

AKA: Brandon James Holland